THIS BOOK IS DEDICATED WITH LOVE
TO NANCY, BOBBIE, AND HAROLD—
WHO ARE NEVER AT A LOSS
FOR A SNAPPY RETORT.

ontents

Introduction *11*

1. **A**round the Round Table *15*

2. **G**etting in the Last Word *23*

3. **D**umbbacks *29*

4. **D**o Re Mi *35*

5. **O**verheard at the White House *41*

6. **K**eeping Score *53*

7. **B**oardroom Badinage *59*

8. **M**ore Stars Than in Heaven *67*

9. **P**rivate Parts *83*

10. **S**hort but Sweet *89*

11. **C**reative Wonders *95*

12. **H**a Ha Ha *111*

13. **C**ourtrooms, Labs, and Battlefields *119*

14. **G**olden Nuggets from the Vast Wasteland *125*

15. **H**ollywood Zingers *135*

16. **L**eaders, Thinkers, Politicians, and
    a Few Scoundrels *143*

   Acknowledgments *159*

   To the Readers *163*

"Frankly,
My Dear..."

Ever wake up in the middle of the night, suddenly and painfully aware of the great retort you could have—should have—made yesterday to your spouse, boss, friend, lawyer, doctor, accountant, salesman, neighbor, child, or that rude delivery guy from the pizza place?

Sure you have. Everyone has. Yet few of us can match the likes of John Kennedy, Winston Churchill, Dorothy Parker, Abraham Lincoln, Groucho Marx, Oscar Wilde, Alfred Hitchcock, or George Bernard Shaw—true masters of the art of spontaneous verbal one-upsmanship.

When a woman boasted to Parker that she had kept her husband "these seven years," Parker didn't congratulate her. "Don't worry," the writer said. "If you keep him long enough, he'll come back in style."

When Stephen Douglas attacked candidate Abraham Lincoln for being two-faced, Lincoln didn't sulk or stammer. "If I had two faces," the future President asked the assembled audience, "would I be wearing this one?"

When Sir Lewis Morris complained—at length—to Oscar Wilde about "a complete conspiracy of silence against me," Wilde knew just what to say. His recommendation: "Join it."

When Dan Quayle compared himself to John Kennedy in the 1988 vice presidential debate, his opponent, Lloyd Bentsen, was ready. "Senator," said Bentsen, "I served with Jack Kennedy. I knew Jack Kennedy. Jack Kennedy was a friend of mine. Senator, you're no Jack Kennedy." It was probably the most memorable comment in the entire campaign. In fact, it may be the only memorable comment in the entire campaign. (Of course, Bentsen still lost, which probably means something.)

The fact is, good comebacks, delivered in a timely way (which means that the solo nighttime variety doesn't count), are some of the greatest verbal pleasures in the world. The pages that follow are full of a few hundred of the best.

They come from the worlds of sports, politics, entertainment, literature, science, law, business, and virtually every other arena of human enterprise. You'll find verbal comebacks from the movies and television, including samplers from *The Honeymooners* and *The Dick Van Dyke Show*. There are exceedingly short retorts (What did Jackie Kennedy intend to feed her new German shepherd dog, she was asked. "Reporters," she said.) They can be poetic, historical, vicious, silly, and even anatomical. (As when Marilyn Monroe was asked by an indelicate interviewer, "Is it true you wear falsies?" "Those who know me better," she answered, "know better.")

Of course, some of the best retorts have dubious heritage. When Charles Lamb was asked how he liked small children, he said, "I like 'em boiled, ma'am, boiled." At least that's what one source claims. Another attributes the same crack to Noël Coward. Yet another contends that it was W. C. Fields who said it. Similarly, collections of the wit of the Algonquin Round Table claim that George S. Kaufman, when asked how he would play a certain bridge hand, answered, "Under an assumed name." But Bennett Cerf—that estimable collector of anecdote—claimed that Hal Sims, the great bridge player said the same thing.

Absent a DNA test for verbiage, there's no way to tell for sure. Maybe it doesn't matter, either. Would *War and Peace* have been less a masterpiece if it was written by David Letterman instead of Leo Tolstoy? Well, maybe, but you get the point.

To paraphrase Shakespeare, the wordplay's the thing.

One warning. You may feel the temptation to follow in the footsteps of the men and women whose words follow. You may discover that, after reading a few dozen choice bits of prose, you want to top your wife or your boss. That's fine. But don't get carried away. Comebacks can be hazardous to your health—and your marriage and job. As Groucho Marx once warned, "When you're always trying for a topper you aren't really listening."

On the other hand, how much is there worth listening to, anyway?

Even if you don't find the personal capacity to match Marx, Wilde, and Parker, don't worry. You can always steal a few of their more obscure comments, and claim them for your own. You won't be the first.

In the meantime, enjoy.

1

Around the Round Table

Some of the members of the Algonquin Round Table are better known today for their witty barbs than for their writing. These sharp-tongued men and women met, informally, six, seven, twelve times a week through the 1920s and 30s to play cards or croquet, eat, drink to excess and mostly talk. Among the charter members of the group were Robert Benchley, George S. Kaufman, Franklin Pierce Adams, and Alexander Woollcott. None, however, was responsible for more comebacks than Dorothy Parker.

When **Dorothy Parker** was informed that the taciturn former President Calvin Coolidge had died, she replied, "How do they know?"

Parker was being debriefed about a cocktail party. "Did you enjoy it?" she was asked.

"Enjoy it?" she responded. "One more drink and I'd have been under the host."

Few men or women ever felt genuinely close to Dorothy Parker. In fact, Helen Thurber, wife of the great humorist James Thurber, was afraid to go to the bathroom when Dorothy Parker was near, for fear that Parker would viciously insult her after she left the room. Parker did, however, have a wonderful relationship with a series of dogs. Once, her pet had an accident in the lobby of the ultraposh Beverly Hills Hotel. "Miss Parker," exclaimed the hotel manager arrogantly, "Look what your dog did."

Dorothy glared back and offered an alternative. "I did it," she told him.

A matronly lady annoyed Parker by boasting of her blissful marriage. Proud of the duration of her wedded bliss, she told Parker, "And I've kept him these seven years."

"Don't worry," responded the writer. "If you keep him long enough, he'll come back in style."

A cab driver refused to allow Dorothy Parker admission to his vehicle. "I'm engaged," he explained.

"Then be happy," she responded.

Harold Ross, the founding editor of *The New Yorker* knew how to run a successful magazine—but for years he had virtually no money to do so. The publication was constantly short on cash and equipment. Once, when Dorothy Parker came into the office, hours after she was expected, Ross questioned his star writer. "What happened to you?" he demanded.

"Somebody was using the pencil," explained Parker innocently.

Another woman—some say it was writer Clare Boothe Luce—allowed Dorothy Parker to sweep in front of her as she was about to enter a restaurant. The writer commented, "Age before beauty," as Parker strode past.

Retorted Parker, "And pearls before swine."

Dorothy Parker had just watched the dress rehearsal of her play *Close Harmony* and was distraught. Her play, she decided, was a wreck. The director, Arthur Hopkins, meanwhile appeared to be absorbed by the chest of actress Wanda Lyon. "Dorothy," he asked. "Don't you think she ought to wear a brassiere in this scene?"

"God no," said Parker. "You've got to have something in the show that moves."

Parker and a number of her writer pals made a West Coast home out of the posh hotel, the Garden of Allah. **Robert Benchley,** who stayed there while he was working on various films and shorts, was the center of every party. On one occasion, he was checking out and was confronted by a doorman whom he had never seen before. The young man pushed a hand in Benchley's way and asked pointedly, "Aren't you going to remember me, sir?"

"Of course," said Benchley smiling. "I'll write you every day."

F. Scott Fitzgerald became somewhat sanctimonious about drinking—only after he went on the wagon himself. "Bob," he righteously addressed Benchley, "Don't you know that drinking is a slow death?"

"So?" replied Benchley, "Who's in a hurry?"

Benchley was leaving a nightclub late one evening, after a few too many drinks. He encountered an epauletted man at the exit, took him to be a doorman, and asked him to hail a taxi cab. The gentleman responded, "I happen to be a rear admiral in the United States Navy."

Benchley was unabashed. "All right then, get us a battleship."

All the Algonquin wits were featured, at one time or another, in a newspaper column written by **Franklin Pierce Adams,** known to all as F.P.A. On one occasion, F.P.A. entered the Algonquin Hotel with amazing news that he couldn't wait to relate. He had just seen Harold Ross, editor of *The New Yorker,* tobogganing.

"Did he look funny?" asked George S. Kaufman.

Adams: "Well, you know how he looks when he's not tobogganing."

Alexander Woollcott, the owl-eyed, snappish writer and radio celebrity, was autographing a new edition of one of his many books. He asked—of no one in particular—"What is so rare as a Woollcott first edition?"

Adams had the answer: "A Woollcott second edition."

Beatrice Kaufman, George S. Kaufman's wife of many years, attended a cocktail party with F.P.A. and sat down on a cane chair. The chair collapsed, leaving Beatrice thoroughly embarrassed, splayed on the floor, captured by the wreck of a chair. Adams looked at her and said, "I've told you a hundred times, Beatrice. That's not funny."

Edna Ferber, author of the novel *Show Boat*, upon which the successful musical was based, was working late into the night with a male collaborator. A pompous hotel clerk, fearful that something immoral was perhaps taking place, called up to the room. "Is there a gentleman in the room?" he inquired.

"I don't know," she told him. "Wait a minute and I'll ask him."

Late one heavy drinking night **George S. Kaufman** confided in some close friends that he was thinking about killing himself.

"How?" they asked.

"With kindness."

Raoul Fleischman's fortune backed *The New Yorker* in its earliest days. He mentioned one night that he was fourteen years old before he knew he was a Jew.

"That's nothing," shot back Kaufman. "I was sixteen before I knew I was a boy."

2

Getting in the Last Word

You wouldn't expect many men or women to come up with memorable conversation just moments or hours before their death. Of course, **Julius Caesar** *was supposed to have uttered the memorable "Et tu, Brute?" ("And you, Brutus?") to his friend and assassin, just before he passed on. But then, that bon mot may have been more a function of Shakespeare's pen than Caesar's lips. Still, a surprising number of memorable comments have been made on various deathbeds of history. Since many of them were later reported by a priest, they have more than the usual amount of historical credibility.*

Henry Thoreau, the great American philosopher, was dying, when a priest asked him if he had made his peace with God.

"I was not aware that we had quarreled," replied Thoreau.

"Why should I talk to you?" asked playwright, con man, real estate salesman, and singer **Wilson Mizner** of a priest, moments before he died. "I've just been talking to your boss."

Heinrich Heine, the German poet, was moments from death, and the priest by his side attempted to comfort him with the thought that God would forgive him for his sins.

"Why of course he will forgive me," replied Heine. "That's his business."

The Italian statesman and writer **Maxximo Taparelli Azeglio** had separated from his second wife Luisa. But in 1866, Luisa heard that her estranged husband was dying and paid him a visit.

"Ah Luisa," he sighed when he saw her enter the room, "you always arrive just as I'm leaving."

Henrik Ibsen, the playwright, never recovered from a debilitating stroke, which he suffered six years before his death. Most of that time was spent lying in bed helpless, cared for by others. One afternoon, his nurse remarked that he seemed to be doing a bit better.

Ibsen was both acrimonious and to the point. "On the contrary," he proclaimed. Then he died.

Aaron Burr, third vice president of the United States and the man who killed Alexander Hamilton in a duel, was on his deathbed.

Just before dawn, his doctor inquired, "Are you prepared to accept salvation?"

Replied the wildly outspoken Burr, "On that subject, I am coy."

John Holmes, a well-known attorney and brother of Supreme Court Justice Oliver Wendell Holmes, was dying. A nurse announced that they would be able to tell when he had died, by feeling his feet. "Nobody ever died with warm feet," she pronounced with the certainty that only a nurse can muster.

"John Rogers did," said Holmes, in his last words.

Rogers, of course, was the Protestant martyr who was killed in 1555, burnt at the stake.

Brendan Behan, the great Irish author, was dying in a London hospital. A visitor asked this rather curious question, "Brendan, do you never think about death?"

Said Behan, "Think about death? Begod man! I'd rather be dead than think about death."

As President **William McKinley** lay dying, his wife Ida cried by his bedside, "I want to go too, I want to go too."

McKinley told her, "We are all going," and those were the last words he spoke.

It appeared as though author **Walter de la Mare** was beginning to recover from a long, life-threatening illness. His daughter asked him as she departed one day whether she could bring him something back on her next trip. Fruit, perhaps, or some flowers?

de la Mare told her, "No no, my dear. Too late for fruit. Too soon for flowers."

3

umbbacks

Some verbal comebacks don't quite make their speakers sound like the brightest buttons. These little unpolished gems remind one of the **James Thurber** *cartoon character, who reclined on a couch with a phone in hand, speaking these immortal words: "Well, if I called the wrong number, why did you answer the phone?"*

One of the victims of the St. Valentine's Day Massacre of 1929—the bloodfest that left Al Capone in absolute control of organized crime—was lying in a dirty pool of blood in a Chicago garage. The police were spraying the dying man with questions about his attackers, desperate to get a little information before he expired.

His response was a true paradigm of the criminal's code: "Nobody shot me," said he.

When President Richard Nixon nominated G. Harrold Carswell to the Supreme Court, opposition was strong and immediate. The Senate approval process was unusually vicious, with many senators alluding to the notion that Carswell was simply not smart enough to sit on the nation's highest court. This led Senator **Roman Hruska** to respond, "Even if

[Carswell is] mediocre, there are a lot of mediocre judges and people and lawyers. They are entitled to a little representation, aren't they?'"

The Hungarian novelist **Ferenc Molnár** responded with great equanimity to the news that his mistress had been unfaithful to him. "She sleeps with others because she loves them," he said. "But for money—only with me!"

A journalist asked an Iraqi official whether his family thought war was coming to that middle eastern nation. "I cannot tell you anything," was the answer. "I am from the Ministry of Information."

Pope Paul VI had just died, and the bulletin came in during a New York Yankee's game. Longtime Yankee player and announcer **Phil Rizzuto** responded to the news: "Well, that kind of puts a damper on even a Yankee win."

The sinking of the *Andrea Doria* was one of the great shipwrecks of all time. After the disaster, Captain **Piero Calamai** stood on the shore, stunned nearly speechless by the tragedy. Reporters clamored around him, asking variations on the same question: "What happened?"
Calamai's simple response: "Somebody sinka my ship."

Nobel Prize–winning astrophysicist William Fowler worked for many years at the Kellogg Radiation Lab, named after the giant manufacturer of corn flakes. He once tried to explain to an elderly woman exactly what he did for a living but had difficulty communicating. "Young man, I still don't know what you do," she complained.

"Well," he answered, attempting to bring the complexities of his work down to the simplest level. "I bust atoms and study how things explode."

"Oh," she said, finally comprehending, "you puff rice!"

Four days after the Watergate burglary, President **Richard Nixon** had grown thoroughly fed up by people who were bothering him about the break-in.

Said he, in response to one comment, "I don't think you're going to see a great, great uproar in this country about the Republican committee trying to bug the Democratic headquarters."

4

Do Re Mi

Singers, composers, and instrumentalists aren't primarily known for their skill with words. Yet some extraordinarily pithy put-downs and retorts have emanated from the lips of divas and other music makers. One of the best known—ascribed to Caruso, Fritz Kreisler, and a handful of others—involves a woman who was giving a large private party and invited the musician to entertain. "My fee is one thousand dollars," explained the entertainer.

"That's fine," said the matron, "but you won't be permitted to socialize with the guests."

"In that case," the musician continued, "my fee is five hundred dollars."

Conductor Karl Böhm was thoroughly impressed with the Swedish soprano **Birgit Nilsson's** work in a Wagner opera. "You are the greatest Brünnhilde I have heard in forty years," he told her.

"Oh," said the diva, "and who did you hear forty years ago?"

George Gershwin may have been one of the greatest composers of popular music in the world, but he still wanted to expand his technical skill in any way he could. While staying in Hollywood, he became acquainted with the older composer, **Arnold Schoenberg,** and asked him to take him on as a student.

Said Schoenberg, "No, I would only make you a bad Schoenberg. And you're such a good Gershwin already."

Jessye Norman, like so many opera singers, used to have Wagnerian proportions. She complained to her host, on one occasion, that she couldn't possibly enter a building through its revolving door.

"Try entering sideways," suggested her companion.

"I have no sideways," explained Norman.

Oblivious to the fact that a well-known composer of the day had died, a friend of **Sir W. S. Gilbert**—of Gilbert and Sullivan fame—asked what the musician was up to.

"He is doing nothing," said Gilbert.

"Surely he is composing?"

"On the contrary," shot back Gilbert, "he is decomposing."

George Martin, record company executive, was explaining in detail precisely how he wanted the Beatles to record their first album for him. "Let me know if there's anything you don't like," he said, summing up.

George Harrison piped up. "Well, for a start, I don't like your tie."

Fyodor Chaliapin, the famed Russian singer, spent the night with a young woman while he was on tour. As he prepared to leave, he offered her two tickets to the opera. They were refused. The girl pointed out that she had no money and needed to buy bread. "If it was bread you wanted," explained the bass, "you should have spent the night with a baker."

Pianist and raconteur **Oscar Levant** had spent an overlong time visiting with George S. Kaufman and his wife. When he finally left, Mrs. Kaufman told Levant that she had saved him from a social faux pas by tipping each of the servants three dollars, telling them that the money came from Levant.

The visitor was not pleased. "You should have given them five!" he complained. "Now, they'll think I'm stingy."

5

Overheard at
the White House

Almost everyone has seen the amazing list of similarities between John Kennedy and Abraham Lincoln—Lincoln's secretary was named Kennedy while Kennedy's was named Lincoln; they both had vice presidents named Johnson; Lincoln was killed in Ford's Theatre and Kennedy was riding in a Ford when he was shot, and on and on. But there's one more, not always mentioned. These two men were unquestionably the two sharpest wordsmiths ever to inhabit the White House. And that's saying something; many of our Presidents, including Lyndon Johnson, Ullyses S. Grant, and even—surprise—Calvin Coolidge came up with a good crack every now and then.

Illinois Senator Stephen A. Douglas attempted to embarrass **Abraham Lincoln** in one of their famous debates by remarking that he had known Lincoln when he was just a storekeeper selling liquor and cigars. "Mr. Lincoln was a very good bartender," Douglas caustically said.

Lincoln replied: "What Mr. Douglas has said is true. I did keep a grocery, and I did sell cotton, candles, and sometimes whiskey. I remember in those days that Mr. Douglas was one of my best customers. Many a time have I stood on one side of the counter and sold whiskey to Mr. Douglas on the other side, but the difference between us now is this: I have left my side of the counter but Mr. Douglas still sticks to his as tenaciously as ever."

On another occasion, Douglas accused Abraham Lincoln of being two-faced. "I leave it to you friends," responded the future president. "If I had two faces, would I be wearing this one?"

The North did rather poorly in the Battle of Bull Run, to put it mildly. After the battle, some military men were explaining to President Lincoln how well the Union had truly fared. After one such self-serving commentary, Lincoln rejoined, "So, it is your notion that we whipped the rebels and then ran away from them?"

The South had seized one of Lincoln's generals along with a dozen military mules. "How unfortunate," said the president. "Those mules cost us two hundred dollars apiece."

In 1846, Abraham Lincoln was running for Congress and attended a sermon delivered by Peter Cartwright, a preacher of the fire and brimstone variety. He asked everyone who wanted to go to heaven to stand up. The congregation arose as one. Except Lincoln. Then, trying another approach, he asked for those who did not want to go to hell to stand up. Lincoln remained sitting. Cartwright, puzzled, said: "If Mr. Lincoln does not want to go to heaven and does not plan to escape hell, perhaps he will tell us where he does want to go."

The answer: "I am going to Congress."

Lincoln never had a great deal of respect for General George B. McClellan, commander of the Union forces. On one occasion, he wired Lincoln: "Have just captured six cows. What shall we do with them?"

Responded the President: "Milk them."

General Joseph Hooker had recently been placed in charge of the army and was anxious for the president to think of him as a man of courage and action. He sent the president a dispatch, which indicated that he was leading his men on horseback. He labeled the message with the words, "Headquarters in the Saddle."

When Lincoln saw the note, he stated, "The trouble with Hooker is that he's got his headquarters where his hindquarters ought to be."

"Mr. President," a voice in the crowd yelled to Abraham Lincoln. "I'm from up in New York State where we believe that God Almighty and Abraham Lincoln are going to save this country."

"My friend," said Lincoln. "You're half right."

A diplomat, visiting the White House, was astonished to find Abraham Lincoln shining his shoes. "Mr. President," exclaimed the diplomat. "Do you black your own shoes?"

"Yes," answered Lincoln. "Whose do you black?"

Abraham Lincoln's Emancipation Proclamation was not a very popular idea among many in positions of power. In fact, when he presented the proposed document to his cabinet, he asked for all those against it to raise their hands. Almost every hand went up. Then, Lincoln called for those in favor. He raised his own hand and proclaimed, "the ayes have it."

John Kennedy asked Russian leader Nikita Krushchev what the medal on his chest represented. The Russian leader explained that it was the Lenin Peace Prize.

Said Kennedy, "I hope you keep it."

When Kennedy attacked Krushchev for never admitting his mistakes, the Soviet leader replied that he had repudiated many of the actions of the Stalin regime in a famous speech before the twentieth Party Congress.

"But those weren't your mistakes," retorted Kennedy.

JFK was disappointed when well-known constitutional law professor Paul Freund told him that he did not intend to leave his long-held post at Harvard to take the job of U.S. solicitor general.

Kennedy: "I'm sorry. I hoped you would prefer making history to writing it."

A reporter asked JFK why he wanted to be president.

The answer was short and sweet. "Because that's where the power is."

JFK was flying on *Air Force One*, chatting with several reporters. One of the reporters asked the president what would happen if their plane were to crash with all aboard.

Said JFK, with a smile, "I'm sure of one thing. Your name would be in the paper the next day. But in very small type."

After being decorated as a military hero, JFK was asked, "How did you become a hero?"

Said he, "It was involuntary. They sank my boat."

Bill Moyers, author and television personality, was press secretary in the Johnson administration. Once the president asked Moyers to begin a meeting of the cabinet with a prayer. Moyers did so, but too quietly for LBJ's taste. "Bill, we couldn't hear you. . . . " complained LBJ.

"I wasn't talking to you, Mr. President," responded Moyers.

President **Ulysses S. Grant** sent a cabinet member out to virtually uncharted western territories, with the instructions, "Write me back and tell me what it is they need out there."

"All this place needs," wired the envoy, "is good people and water."

Grant wired back: "That is all hell needs."

When George Bush was still a congressman, he asked President **Lyndon Johnson** whether he should run for Senate.

Replied Johnson: "The difference between being a member of the Senate and a member of the House is the difference between chicken salad and chicken shit."

President **Ronald Reagan** had just been shot and was being rushed into emergency surgery. He was surrounded by medical men and women, who were assuring him that all would be well soon.

The president looked up with a simple inquiry, "Please assure me that you are all Republicans."

During the course of debates between Ronald Reagan and incumbent Jimmy Carter, Reagan made a reference to an approaching depression. Carter thought he'd caught him in a gaffe. "That shows how much he knows," he retorted. "This is a recession."

Reagan was undeterred: "If the president wants a definition, I'll give him one. Recession is when your neighbor loses his job, depression is when you lose yours. And recovery will be when Jimmy Carter loses his."

Thomas Jefferson had just taken over for Ben Franklin as U.S. minister to France. He was met by the French prime minister who asked, "Have you come to replace Dr. Franklin?"

Jefferson: "No one could ever replace Benjamin Franklin. I am only succeeding him."

At a dinner featuring many important political figures, railroad executive Chauncey Depew took a cheap shot at **William Howard Taft's** size. He glanced at Taft's ample mid-section and inquired what he planned to call the child when it was born.

Later, when it was Taft's turn to speak, he had the absolute last word: "If it's a girl, I shall name it for my wife. If it's a boy, I will call him Junior. But if it is, as I suspect, just gas, I will call it Chauncey Depew."

Herbert Hoover was making efforts to get the country's economy moving again—with little success. Meanwhile, the newspapers were increasingly critical. Former President Calvin Coolidge tried to put Hoover's mind at rest with a bit of farmhouse wisdom. "You can't expect to see calves running in the field the day after you put the bull to the cows," he said.

"No," replied Hoover, "but I would at least expect to see contented cows."

A woman was sitting next to the famously quiet **Calvin Coolidge** at dinner and tried to persuade him to chat. "I have a bet," she said, "that I can get you to say more than two words."

"You lose," Coolidge advised.

In an effort to amuse President Coolidge, a senator pointed to the White House on a walk around the grounds and asked, "I wonder who lives there."

"Nobody," Coolidge responded, "They just come and go."

A visitor observed that he couldn't understand how **Franklin**

Delano Roosevelt could possibly be so patient with American politics, and the president answered: "If you had spent two years trying to get a slight movement in your toe, and then tasted the triumph of having it actually move, you, too, would learn something about patience."

Eleanor Roosevelt was continually traveling, visiting various sites around the United States. One morning, FDR arose, unsure as to exactly where his wife was that day. Malvina Thompson, Eleanor's secretary, filled him in: "She's in prison, Mr. President."

"I'm not surprised," said FDR, "but what for?"

6

Keeping Score

Despite the fact that professional athletes aren't widely known for their verbal skills, some of the most common-sensical retorts of all time come from baseball players, boxers, and other game players. Consider baseball great **Waite Hoyt's** *comment at Babe Ruth's funeral. Fellow athlete Joe Dugan had just lamented, "Lord, I'd give my right arm for an ice-cold beer."*

Replied Hoyt: "Joe, so would the Babe."

Darryl Strawberry's career was falling apart as he was found to have substance abuse problems. His manager, **Tommy Lasorda** of the Los Angeles Dodgers, lost all patience with Strawberry. When a caller to a cable TV talk show suggested that Strawberry was "a dog," Lasorda corrected him. "You're wrong. Darryl Strawberry is not a dog. A dog is loyal and runs hard after balls."

Dizzy Dean, the great ball player-turned-baseball announcer, was not a grammarian. During the Depression years, a critic accused him of leading young people to use improper English. Dean responded, "A lot of folks that ain't saying ain't ain't eating."

"Oh Joe," Marilyn gushed to her new husband, **Joe DiMaggio,** after a triumphant tour of American Army bases, "it was so exciting. The boys were thrilled. You have never heard such cheers."

The soft-spoken DiMaggio murmured, "Yes I have."

Larry Cole was the misbegotten Dallas Cowboys offensive end who played for eleven successive seasons without a single touchdown. Finally, he planted one firmly behind the goal posts and naturally was subject to questions about his long scoreless streak.

"Anyone can have a dry decade," said he.

Joe Louis, heavyweight champion of the world, was defending his title against Billy Conn, a speedy, tricky boxer. Conn's strength was his ability to quickly move in, jab, and uppercut and then get out of his opponent's way.

Louis was unafraid when all these strengths were pointed out to him. "He can run," said the slugger, "but he can't hide."

Muhammad Ali was riding a commercial airline and was told by the stewardess that it was time, please, to fasten his safety belt.

"Superman don't need no seat belt," argued Ali.

"Superman don't need no airplane either," replied the stewardess.

When Isaac Stern the violinist met **Muhammad Ali,** Stern observed to the boxer, "You might say we're in the same business. We both earn a living with our hands."

Remarked the boxer, "You must be pretty good. There isn't a mark on you."

Lefty Gomez was one of the greatest pitchers in Yankee history. He won twenty-six games and lost five in 1934. But as he grew older, he lost his touch. "I don't think you're throwing as hard as you need to," manager Joe McCarthy told him.

"You're wrong, Joe," Gomez said. "I'm throwing twice as hard. But the ball isn't going as fast."

Dodgers Pitcher **Billy Loes** wasn't impressed by the idea that he should buy life insurance for his parents, both of whom he was supporting.

"They wouldn't need it," said he. "If anything happened to me, it would kill them."

Shaquille O'Neal, star of the Orlando Magic, was at the foul line when he heard A. C. Green trying to throw his shot off. Green, a co-founder of Athletes for Abstinence, shouted, "You'll be all right as soon as you get some experience."

Shaq shot back, "And you'll be okay as soon as you get some sex."

In 1930, **Babe Ruth** was told by a newspaper reporter that he was then making more money than the President of the United States.

Ruth was unfazed. "But I had a better year," he said.

A reporter asked basketball star **Charles Barkley** what he would do with himself if he retired.

Said Barkley, "If push came to shove I could lose all self-respect and become a reporter."

Hank Aaron, who holds the record for most home runs hit in a career, was at bat in the 1957 World Series, when the catcher Yogi Berra told him he was holding the bat in the wrong position—tradition holds that the batter should be able to see the trademark. "Turn it around," he said.

Aaron had other things on his mind. "Didn't come up here to read," he told Berra. "Came up here to hit."

7
Boardroom
Badinage

Barry Diller, *media mogul, met with unaccustomed defeat in his efforts to take over Paramount Communications in 1994. Would he make another bid for the giant firm? Would he litigate? Did he have a next step planned? These were the questions Diller was assaulted by. His response was straightforward: "They won," he said. "We lost. Next." Other business people have been similarly direct.*

Warren Buffet, the so-called Sage of Omaha, is one of the most successful investors in history. *Forbes* magazine once proclaimed that he possessed more wealth than any other American. "Now that you've become the richest man in the country, what is your next goal?" a shareholder asked him.

"To be the oldest," was his reply.

Nathan Mayer, Lord Rothschild, was one of the richest men in Europe. So it was no surprise that a hansom cab driver complained about his tip, explaining that: "Your Lordship's son always gives me a good deal more than this."

"I dare say he does," Rothschild said. "But then, he has a rich father and I haven't."

Frank Gilbreth, one of the nation's top efficiency experts, used to travel extensively with his large brood of children. Passersby would ask, "How do you feed all those kids?"

His answer—later immortalized as the title of the book about his life, written by two of his children—"They come cheaper by the dozen, you know."

Robber baron and railroad magnate **William H. Vanderbilt** was asked to consider polling his customers to see if they thought it was a good idea to put luxury trains on his line.

His priorities were clear. Said Vanderbilt: "The public be damned."

Publisher **William Randolph Hearst** had been editorializing in favor of Cuban independence from the Spanish for some time. He anticipated that there would soon be some bloody violence to fill the pages of his newspaper. So he dispatched artist Frederic Remington to Havana to send back pictures of the action. But to Hearst's great disappointment, relative calm prevailed.

Remington wired: "Everything is quiet. There is no trouble here. There will be no war. I wish to return."

Hearst responded by wire: "Please remain. You furnish the pictures, and I'll furnish the war."

"There's money in the movies," said a friend to Hearst, who had lost vast sums on a series of flops.

"Yes," agreed Hearst. "Mine."

Hearst was sometimes a trifle blunt in his business dealings. He decided that perhaps he'd like to buy *The New York Tribune* and wired Whitelaw Reid, the paper's owner, this terse message: "How much will you take for *The Tribune?*"

The answer, by return wire: "Three cents on weekdays. Five cents on Sundays."

Hearst had an odd approach to money matters. His business manager was startled when he didn't fire an employee who, it was discovered, had been embezzling money. Why not?

"I have a new understanding with him," Hearst explained. "He is to steal only small sums hereafter. The largest are to come to me."

After millionaire businessman J. P. Morgan announced, "America is good enough for me," Presidential candidate **William Jennings**

Bryan rejoindered, "Whenever he doesn't like it, he can give it back to us."

J. P. Morgan was asked what he thought would happen to the stock market. No one, to be sure, was in a better position to know than the founder of J. P. Morgan & Co. Said he, accurately, "It will fluctuate."

Philip K. Wrigley had taken over for his father in running the chewing-gum company that still bears the family name. Once, on an airplane, his seat mate inquired as to why it was necessary to spend millions on advertising when everyone already knew the company's products well.

"For the same reason the pilot of this plane keeps the engine running when we're already twenty-nine thousand feet up," was Wrigley's reply.

United Auto Workers president **Walter Reuther** was walking through a Ford plant with a company executive. The Ford official pointed at one of the shiny new robots the firm was using and asked, "How are you union people going to collect union dues from these guys?"

Reuther's reply was equally pointed: "And how are you going to get them to buy Fords?"

James Thomas Aubrey was the president of CBS in the early 1960s. He was known as a courageous loner, with no fear of anything—personally or professionally. On one occasion he was flying out of New York and another CBS executive noticed that one of the plane's engines was on fire. He woke Aubrey to inform him of this alarming turn of events.

"God damn it," the still drowsy Aubrey responded. "Don't wake me up again until all four are on fire."

John Gates was a turn-of-the-century robber baron and contemporary of Andrew Carnegie. He was given to long reminiscences. He began telling a story, "I went into steel. . . ." when he was interrupted by **Isaac L. Ellwood,** another immensely successful businessman and the inventor of barbed wire.

"How do you spell that?" Ellwood wanted to know.

8

More Stars Than in Heaven

Stars of radio, stage, screen, and television sometimes develop a reputation for brilliant wordplay based on the backs of their writers. Some of the choicest bon mots ever uttered by the likes of Bob Hope and George Burns were bought and paid for by the stars. That said, an astonishing number of men and women connected with the entertainment business go down in the Verbal Comeback Hall of Fame. The list is topped with the likes of immortals Groucho Marx, Alfred Hitchcock, and Tallulah Bankhead and runs through to contemporary celebrities like Robin Williams and Mel Brooks.

A contestant on *You Bet Your Life* told host **Groucho Marx** that she was "approaching forty."

"From which direction?" asked Groucho.

Director Sam Wood was trying to direct the Marx Brothers. That was much like trying to direct a cyclone in Kansas. The task was made all the harder in this instance by the fact that none of the brothers had any respect for their boss.

"You can't make an actor out of clay," the director told the brothers one particularly acrimonious day.

"Nor a director out of Wood," exclaimed Groucho.

"Will there always be a Groucho?" an interviewer asked the comedian.

"There'll always be a Groucho, just as there will always be an England. Although lately, England hasn't been doing so well."

Groucho was told that his son, Arthur, would not be permitted to swim in a "no-Jews-allowed" country club. He immediately sat down and wrote the president of the club.

"Since my little son is only half-Jewish, would it be all right if he goes into the pool only up to his waist?"

Groucho Marx was riding down in an elevator with television personality Dick Cavett. Two priests boarded, who immediately recognized the great comedian. "My mother was a tremendous fan of yours for years," exulted one.

"Oh really?" asked Groucho, not missing a beat. "I didn't know you fellows were allowed to have mothers."

Like Groucho Marx, **W. C. Fields** was often at odds with his studio. One particularly unpleasant disagreement resulted in the comedian's leaving the studio to sulk. He waited in his mansion for concessions, which didn't come. Finally, Louis B. Mayer, the studio's chief (the final M in MGM), personally visited the Fields's household.

The butler was stunned. "It's Mr. Mayer himself," he told Fields. "What shall I say to him?"

Fields answered in his familiar gravelly drawl. "Give him an evasive answer. . . . Tell him to go fuck himself."

Charlie Mack was a well-known vaudeville star, half of the team Moran and Mack. He had fallen desperately behind on his alimony payments and was thrown in jail. He turned to old buddy W. C. Fields: "Please send me five hundred dollars. I'm in jail up here," wired Mack.

"If it's a good jail, I'll join you," responded Fields.

Alfred Hitchcock was insistent that he never view his films in a theater with a real audience. "But don't you miss hearing them scream?" he was asked.

"No," said the director, "I can hear them when I'm making the picture."

After witnessing the terrifying shower scene in *Psycho*, a viewer wrote to Alfred Hitchcock to complain. His wife, it seemed, was now afraid to take a shower. Did Hitchcock have any advice?

"Have you ever considered sending your wife to the dry cleaner?" he suggested.

"Which would you say is my best side, Mr. Hitchcock?" actress Mary Anderson asked the great director when posing for photographs for the 1944 film *Lifeboat*.

"My dear, you're sitting on it," he replied.

Also during the shooting of *Lifeboat*, Hitchcock told star **Tallulah Bankhead,** "We'll shoot you through gauze. It will make you look better."

Bankhead responded, "To make me look better you'll have to shoot me through linoleum."

The famous columnist Earl Wilson once asked the husky-voiced Tallulah Bankhead, "Have you ever been mistaken for a man?"

Replied Bankhead, "No, darling, have you?"

Oscar Wilde and **Sarah Bernhardt** were in the midst of a vitriolic argument.

"Do you mind if I smoke, madam?" he asked.

"I don't care if you burn," said Bernhardt.

Bernhardt suffered a tragic accident when she was playing in *La Tosca,* causing one of her legs to be amputated ten years later. Soon after, she received a request from the manager of the Pan-American Exposition to exhibit her leg—for a $100,000 fee.

Bernhardt had one question, which she wired back: "Which leg?"

Sarah Bernhardt inadvertently committed a major social faux pas when she seated a well-known banker, who was recently divorced, directly across from his ex-wife at a dinner party. She took the bull by the horns.

"You two have just been divorced, haven't you?" she asked. "What a lot you must have to tell each other."

Carol Burnett's coat got caught in the closing door of a New York City taxicab. Typically, the driver didn't even notice and drove on, with the comedienne running alongside the cab. Luckily, a passing woman noticed the situation and hailed the cab, which stopped. Burnett opened the door and the driver realized what had happened. "Are you all right?" he asked.

"Yes," said she. "But how much more do I owe you?"

A *Newsweek* reporter asked **Mel Brooks** what he thought of critics and Brooks either misheard or pretended to. His answer: "You can't sleep in the country because of them."

The interviewer realized the source of the confusion and corrected Brooks: "I think that's crickets you're talking about sir. I meant critics."

Brooks: "Oh, critics. They're no good."

Interviewer: "Why is that?"

Brooks: "They can't make music with their legs."

"A couple of gals in the reception room," announced an usher to **Ethel Barrymore** one day, "who say they went to school with you. What shall I do?"

"Wheel them in."

"May I do *Candida?*" actress **Cornelia Otis Skinner** wired playwright **George Bernhard Shaw.**

"Excellent. Greatest!" wired back Shaw.

Skinner: "Undeserving such praise."

Shaw: "I meant the play."
Skinner: "So did I."

Robin Williams was swept away by the barrage of compliments which greeted him at a black-tie dinner in his honor.

"God!" he exclaimed. "I sound like a breath mint."

When Fanny Brice wanted tickets to one of **Billy Rose's** shows, she inquired by telegram: "Have you two openings down there?"

Rose responded: "Yes, my giant quit and my trained snake died."

Katharine Hepburn was first meeting her future collaborator and the love of her life, Spencer Tracy, in 1941, on the set of *Woman of the Year*. Producer **Joe Mankiewicz** was doing the introductions. The statuesque Hepburn gazed at the moderately tall Tracy and asked, "You're rather short, aren't you?"

Mankiewicz responded for him: "Don't worry, honey. He'll cut you down to size."

Early in their series of films, **Spencer Tracy** demanded that he be given top billing over Katharine Hepburn. This created something of a stir at the studio, and executives were dispatched to talk him out of it. "Don't forget the law of the sea," one studio boss suggested. "Ladies first."

"This is a movie," snapped Tracy. "Not a lifeboat."

Norma Talmadge was one of the greatest of the silent film stars. But she just wasn't cut out for the talkies. She made two sound films, both of which were rejected by moviegoers from coast to coast. So Talmadge retired to enjoy her vast accumulated wealth and was swiftly consigned to the back lot of film history.

A few years later, a fan stopped her on the street asking, "May I have your autograph?"

"Get away dear," the former star shrugged, "I don't need you any more."

Carrie Fisher started her career as an actress—notably by leading the forces of good in the *Star Wars* films. But she became a successful novelist and screenwriter as well. "Gee," a friend commented, "it must be great now that you are a writer. Now you get to call the shots."

"Not really," advised Fisher, "but at least I get to fill some of the syringes."

Fred Allen was complaining to the owner of the Stage Deli. "Your food is very good, but it gave me heartburn."

The response: "So, what did you expect in a delicatessen? Sunburn?"

Hackaliah Bailey was one of the originators of the modern-day circus, although he was no relation to the man who was ultimately to become partners with P. T. Barnum. Early in his career, this Bailey owned half interest in an elephant. The other half was owned by a somewhat unscrupulous individual who refused to cough up Bailey's share of the profits.

Bailey resolved this problem by lifting a gun to the elephant's shoulder and threatening to shoot.

"Hey," the partner shouted. "That's half my elephant!"

"I'm only aiming at my half," Bailey responded.

For some time, **P. T. Barnum** exhibited a baboon, claiming it was a gorilla that had the strength to bend "the heavy iron bars of his cage." When a professor from the Smithsonian Institution saw the exhibit, he told Barnum in confidence, "He is a very fine specimen of a baboon, but he is no gorilla."

"What is the reason he is not a gorilla?" Barnum inquired.

"Real gorillas have no tails."

Barnum was unfazed: "I know that ordinary gorillas have no tails, but mine has and that makes the specimen more remarkable."

Well-connected press agent Emmett Davis had taken his mother to a fancy New York party at Gracie Mansion, the mayor's home. Davis promised his mother that there would be celebrities aplenty there, but none seemed to be in attendance.

Finally, like a cat bringing a mouse to its master, Davis pointed out that Jole Gabor, Zsa Zsa's mother, had walked in. Mom Davis had never heard of the Gabors and indicated as much to actress **Lisa Ferraday,** who had accompanied them to the party.

"Mrs. Davis," said Ferraday. "Not to know the Gabors personally already is a luxury. But not to know who they are . . . my God, how I envy you."

Mae West was taking all the best lines in a film for herself. Director Ernst Lubitsch pointed out that this wasn't the best thing for the project; the most successful films had two strong characters, not just one. "Look at *Romeo and Juliet*," he said.

"Let Shakespeare do it his way," cracked West. "I'll do it mine. We'll see who comes out better."

John Gilbert, a film star of the silent era, married Broadway star Ina Claire. A reporter walked up to the couple and asked Claire how it felt to be married to a celebrity. "Why don't you ask my husband?" she rejoindered.

It was during a major newspaper strike in New York City that rumors flew that **Bette Davis** had died. When the actress was apprised of the rumor she responded, "With the newspaper strike on, I wouldn't consider it."

Marilyn Monroe discussed the Stanislavsky method of acting for over ten minutes on a radio program. A critic later attacked her press agent—accusing him of having written a script for Monroe, which she simply mouthed.

Her agent's reply: "What press agent knows that much about Stanislavsky?"

Gertrude Lawrence was not thrilled with the lines she was given in the Noël Coward play, *Private Lives*. She wired him the following: "Nothing wrong that can't be fixed."

Coward responded: "Nothing to be fixed except your performance."

Sol Hurok was attending a screening of *Tonight We Sing*, a biographical film about the impresario's life. One of the themes of the film was that Hurok and his wife were never able to go on their honeymoon because some calamity involving his famous clients always interfered.

Hurok was enchanted with the picture and turned to his wife Emma. "Emitchka, Emitchka. We have to go on that honeymoon," he told her, swept away with emotion.

"Sol, Sol, Sol," came the response. "That movie was about your first wife!"

D. W. Griffith, one of the greats of the early days of film, was well into retirement by the time *Gone With the Wind* opened in 1939. When he saw the incredible expense and effort that went into the scene that featured hundreds of sick and dying soldiers in an army hospital, Griffith commented, "I got the same effect with a close-up of a few corpses."

Fred Zinnemann, though not a household name, directed a long list of important feature films and was the recipient of two Oscars for film direction (for *From Here to Eternity* and *A Man for All Seasons*.) When a relative neophyte in one of Hollywood's big studios met with Zinnemann, he should have known—but clearly did not—to whom he was speaking.

"Tell me about yourself, Mr. Zinnemann," asked the ignorant young fellow.

Zinnemann didn't storm from the room in a show of Hollywood vanity. "You first," he asked.

9

Private Parts

"In olden days," opined Cole Porter, "a glimpse of stocking was looked on as something shocking." A little—or a lot—of skin has not only shocked, but been the source for some witty and wildly spontaneous quips.

A reporter was discussing a nude photo of **Marilyn Monroe** with the actress. He inquired as to whether she had anything on at all.

Monroe was quick. "Oh yes," she said. "I had the radio on."

Marilyn Monroe was asked by an indelicate reviewer. "Is it true you wear falsies?"

Her reply: "Those who know me better . . . know better."

When actor Donald Sutherland first met **Tallulah Bankhead,** it was under somewhat unusual circumstances. The actress had entered his dressing room completely naked. He stared, and she responded, "What's the matter darling? Haven't you ever seen a blond before?"

Truman Capote was drinking with friends at a Key West bar. A woman, somewhat sloshed, came up to the famous author and asked him to autograph a napkin she held in her hand.

Her husband, drunker than she, was inexplicably outraged by the scene. He stumbled over, unzipped his pants, made his private parts public and said, "Since you're autographing things, why don't you autograph this?"

The room grew silent as Capote responded, "I don't know if I can autograph it, but perhaps I can initial it."

Sir John Gielgud announced to his fellow male cast members that men wearing leotards must wear jock straps on the stage.

"Please Sir John," inquired one. "Does that apply to us who only have small parts?"

Britain's Labor Party, led by Clement Attlee, was busy nationalizing industries. Attlee encountered former prime minister **Winston Churchill** in the men's room and noted that Churchill had chosen to use the urinal farthest away from the one at which he was temporarily stationed.

"A bit standoffish today?" inquired Attlee.

"That's right," said Churchill. "Because every time you see something big, you want to nationalize it."

Winston Churchill was visiting with FDR at the White House and was surprised when the president came rolling into his room in a wheelchair, thoroughly unannounced. Actually, the president was even more surprised as the prime minister was totally nude. Churchill may have been without apparel, but he was never without words. "You see sir," he said, "I have always told you that the prime minister has nothing to conceal from the president of the United States."

Churchill was startled when his American hostess, who was serving chicken, corrected his request for some breast. "In this country," she explained, "we ask for white meat or dark meat." The next day, Churchill sent her an orchid with a note that read, "I would be most obliged if you would pin this on your white meat."

During the years when **Benjamin Franklin** served as minister to France, the fashion for high-toned ladies was to wear their gowns very low-cut. King Louis XVI took note of one woman with very little in the cleavage department and pointed her out to Franklin. "It's a pity," he said, "she does not do justice to her décolletage. God did not endow her."

Franklin agreed, but went on, "You sire, on the other hand, can endow us. For our government in Philadelphia, like the unfortunate lady in question, has the same problem. An uncovered deficit."

Salmon Chase was chief justice of the Supreme Court as well as secretary of the treasury under Lincoln. His picture is on the $10,000 bill. When he met an impressively attractive young woman from the south, she coyly told him, "I must warn you that I'm an unreconstructed rebel."

Said Chase, "In your case madam, reconstruction—even in the slightest degree—would be nothing short of sacrilege."

10

Short but Sweet

Retorts don't have to be long. In fact, some of the pithiest com-
ments ever consisted of no more than a single word. Perhaps the most ex-
treme example of this particular art was committed to paper. Victor Hugo
had sent his manuscript of Les Miserables *to his publishers and heard no*
response. So he sent them an extremely short note, which read entirely as
follows: "?"

The publisher's response: "!"

Jackie Kennedy, then first lady, was being interviewed about her newly acquired German shepherd puppy. "What do you intend to feed it?" one insightful reporter inquired.

Said Jackie, "Reporters."

Before **Lawrence Eagleburger** took over as acting secretary of state, he was asked how he planned to run the state department with James Baker gone.

The answer: "Badly."

A radio interviewer in London asked **Woody Allen,** "You're a film director, a musician, a scriptwriter, an actor, and a comedian. Which of these roles do you prefer?"

"Yes," answered Allen.

One of **Lyndon Johnson**'s daughters was asked by a reporter to describe her relationship with her dad.

The answer came quickly. "Blood," she said.

Samuel Gompers, early labor leader and first president of the American Federation of Labor, was clear in his views. He was asked what were the main goals of unions.

"More," he said.

Alfred Hitchcock was confronted by a pompous French customs inspector at the airport in Paris. Upon scrutinizing Hitchcock's passport, which listed his profession as "producer," the customs official asked, "And what do you produce?"

Hitchcock responded, "Gooseflesh."

Gunter Schabowski, one-time party boss of East Berlin, was asked if the Communists could ever lose a "free, general, democratic, and secret election."

His caustic, though prophetic answer: "Theoretically."

Barbara Bush, responding to allegations that her husband the president had been unfaithful to her: "Baloney."

Anthony Clement McAuliffe commanded the 101st Airborne Division during World War II. He was completely surrounded. He was outnumbered four to one by the Germans. The enemy sent word that they would accept his surrender.

McAuliffe's reply: "Nuts."

Bubar Gulbenkian was a British philanthropist who inherited vast sums of money from his father. Once, he was filling out a survey, which inquired: "Position in Life."

His response: "Enviable."

A British journalist from a well-known newspaper walked up to **Noël Coward** and inquired, "Mr. Coward, would you like to say something to *The Star?*"

Replied Coward, "Twinkle!"

Father Agnellus Andrew was a famed British clergyman, who for years advised the BBC about Roman Catholic issues. One producer wrote him to ask how he could establish the precise and official Roman Catholic position about heaven and hell.

The Father sent back his reply: "Die."

Donna Reed (who played Donna Stone on the highly successful sitcom that bore her name) was asked, years after her show was a major success, what television had given her.

Reed: "Money."

Darryl Zanuck, producer of such great films as *The Grapes of Wrath*, *Gentleman's Agreement*, and *The Longest Day* was departing France. He was required to fill out an "exit form" for the passport office. One of the blanks left to be filled in was for "Occupation."

Zanuck's answer: "Idiot."

11

Creative Wonders

When literary figures reach a certain critical mass appeal, a strange phenomenon occurs: they begin to find that it doesn't matter who comes up with a wonderful quip—it's attributed to them. This phenomenon, in part, explains why Mark Twain, Oscar Wilde, and George Bernard Shaw have been credited with more great lines than any three men could possibly generate. Take for example, the story of the man who heard that Twain received a dollar a word for his writing and mailed him a dollar with the request to "send . . . a word." By return mail the man received the reply: "Thanks." Great story, except for the fact that it's also attributed to Rudyard Kipling.

"You Missouri people are all right," a New Yorker told **Mark Twain.** "But you're too provincial."

"Provincial?" shot back Twain. "On the contrary, nobody in New York knows anything about Missouri, but everybody in Missouri knows all about New York."

"I'll wager you can't cite a single passage in the Bible which forbids polygamy," a Mormon who was advocating the benefits of multiple wives challenged Mark Twain.

"Sure I can," responded Twain. "No man can serve two masters."

Early in his career, before he became famous, Mark Twain was the editor of a tiny Missouri newspaper. A reader once wrote to inform Twain that a spider had arrived folded into his newspaper and to find out whether Twain thought this was a positive or negative omen.

Twain replied: "Dear Subscriber. Finding a spider in your paper was neither good luck nor bad luck for you. The spider was merely looking over our paper to see which merchant is not advertising so that he can go to that store, spin his web across the door, and lead a life of undisturbed peace ever afterward."

The hostess at a dinner party complained to Mark Twain because he had not weighed into a passionate discussion about heaven and hell.

"Madam you must excuse me," said Twain. "I am silent because of necessity. I have friends in both places."

Mark Twain was thoroughly agitated one day when he was trapped on a slow, late train. When the conductor made his rounds, asking for the fare, Twain handed him half the required amount—a child's rate.

"Are you a child?" the conductor asked, facetiously.

"No, not any more," Twain responded with a glare. "But I was when I got on your damn train."

While visiting the capital of Virginia, Mark Twain developed severe pains in his gut. "It can't be the air or the food you ate in Richmond," a native protested. "There's no healthier city in America than Richmond. Our death rate is only one person per day."

"Run over to the newspaper office," said Twain, "and find out if today's victim has died yet."

Mark Twain had just finished speaking to an appreciative crowd when famed attorney William M. Evarts arose, his hands in his pockets, to gibe: "Does it not seem unusual to this gathering that a professional humorist should really appear funny?"

Twain responded: "Does it not also appear strange to this assembly that a lawyer should have his hands in his own pockets?"

"Have you anything to declare?" a customs official asked **Oscar Wilde.**

"No, I have nothing to declare." A pause. "Except my genius."

As a young man at Oxford, Oscar Wilde was being tested on his ability to translate from the Greek. The assignment was to orally translate the Greek version of the New Testament, and Wilde began accurately translating the story of the Passion. His examiners told him that he had passed and could stop, but Wilde went on reading. They again interrupted, but Wilde continued translating. Finally, they got him to cease and asked why he was so insistent on continuing.

"Oh, do let me go on," Wilde said. "I want to see how it ends."

"It is a complete conspiracy of silence against me," Sir Lewis Morris complained to Oscar Wilde. "A conspiracy of silence! What ought I to do, Oscar?"

Wilde's recommendation: "Join it."

Oscar Wilde had already become a well-known author when George Bernard Shaw was just starting out. The two men met, and Shaw held forth for some time about a new magazine he intended to start. Finally, Wilde said, "You haven't told us the title of your magazine."

"Oh, as for that," Shaw answered. "What I'd want to do would be to impress my own personality on the public. I'd call it Shaw's Magazine: Shaw Shaw Shaw."

"Yes," responded Wilde, "And how would you spell it?"

The Theatre Guild wired **George Bernard Shaw** with the following: "Please alter fourth act of *Saint Joan* so commuters can catch last train to suburbs."

Shaw's response: "Alter the trains."

The opening night of Shaw's *Arms and the Man* was a great success. Shaw came out in front of the curtain and was royally greeted by the cheering crowd. Then, as the joyous response dulled, a single hiss—loud and clear—came from the depths of the audience. Shaw bowed in the direction of the sound and stated clearly, "I quite agree with you sir, but what can two do against so many?"

George Bernard Shaw once attended a performance by a string quartet. During the intermission, his companion remarked, "These men have been playing together for twelve years."

"Surely," said Shaw, "we have been here longer than that."

Film star Danny Kaye told Shaw, "You're a young-looking ninety," and was surprised when Shaw didn't accept the compliment warmly.

"Nonsense," argued the cantankerous writer. "I look exactly like a man of ninety should look. Everyone else looks older because of the dissolute lives they lead."

Famed dancer Isadora Duncan was known for many attributes—some of them purely physical in nature. She informed George Bernard Shaw that she had come upon the wonderful notion that they should conceive a child together. "With my body and your brains, what a wonder it would be," she explained.

"Yes," responded Shaw, "but what if it had my body and your brains?"

A young fellow with little sense once told **Samuel Johnson** that a good cook seemed to him to have more value than all the poets that ever lived. Responded Johnson, "Sir, in that opinion you have the support of every dog in town."

Boswell's *Life of Johnson* describes an episode in which Samuel Johnson was arguing at length with a gentleman. After Johnson made a powerful point, he was told, "I don't understand you sir."

Johnson was thoroughly irritated by obtuseness. "I have found you an argument," he said. "I am not obliged to find you an understanding."

Carl Sandburg attended the rehearsal of a play as a favor to a young playwright. He promptly fell asleep. The writer was crushed. "How could you sleep when you knew I wanted your opinion?" he asked.

"Young man," said Sandburg, "sleep is an opinion."

"Have you read *Gone With the Wind?*" asked a with-it young woman of longtime Columbia professor **Raymond Weaver** in 1936.

"No," said the professor.

"Well, you ought to. It's been out six months."

Now, it was the professor's turn. "Have you read the *Divine Comedy?*"

"No."

"Well, you ought to. It's been out six hundred years."

Thomas Campbell, the Scottish poet, was attending a dinner and was asked to give a toast to the assembled, most of whom were writers. He began to toast the health of Napoleon Bonaparte and found that the crowd would not allow him to continue. Napoleon, at that point in time, was the enemy of the British.

Campbell responded to the hubbub with eloquence. "Gentlemen," he explained, "you must not mistake me. I admit that the French emperor is a tyrant. I admit that he is a monster. I admit that he is the sworn foe of our nation and, if you will, of the whole human race. But, gentlemen, we must be just to our great enemy. We must not forget that he once shot a bookseller."

"Sir James Barrie, I presume?" began a newspaper reporter attempting to interview *Peter Pan* author **J. M. Barrie.**

Before shutting the door in his face, Barrie had just two words to say: "You do."

"I believe, **Charles Lamb,** that you have heard me preach?" asked Sir Samuel Coleridge, in the midst of a lengthy and rambling diatribe.

Responded Lamb, "I never heard you do anything else."

Clark Gable found himself in the company of author **William Faulkner** and asked him who he thought were the five greatest authors of the day. Faulkner easily responded: "Hemingway, Cather, Mann, Dos Passos, and myself."

"Oh," asked Gable facetiously, "do you write for a living?"

"Yes," said Faulkner. "And what do you do?"

Journalist **John Gunther** road to international fame on the basis of his series of *Inside* books, like *Inside Russia* and *Inside Africa*. Interviewer Clifton Fadiman asked him, "What will you do when you run out of continents?"

Gunther replied, "Try incontinence."

Quentin Crisp, the author of *The Naked Civil Servant*, told an ill-mannered lout who attacked him for his colorful appearance: "You cannot bother me sir. I am one of the stately homos of England."

Sir Arthur Conan Doyle, who wrote the *Sherlock Holmes* stories, was a great believer in spiritualism and the ability of mediums to contact the dear departed. A friend of his was taken seriously ill, and it was recommended that Doyle visit immediately.

"I'll call him tomorrow," Doyle promised.

"That may be too late."

"Then I'll speak to him next week."

George Bernard Shaw was tall and thin, and **G. K. Chesterton,** the British writer, was quite the opposite. "If I were as fat as you, I'd hang myself," Shaw told his rotund friend.

"And if I had it in my mind to hang myself," came back Chesterton, "I'd use you as the rope."

An editor at publishing house Harcourt Brace asked **T. S. Eliot** whether he thought that most editors are failed writers.

Eliot's response: "Perhaps, but so are most writers."

"You don't know me," said an unknown man to writer **Hilaire Belloc.**

"Yes I do," said Belloc, walking away.

French writer **Voltaire** attended an orgy and was invited back to join the group the next night.

He replied, "Once a philosopher; twice a pervert!"

Alfred, Lord Tennyson was told that a particular marriage had been a mistake; that the couple in question might have been thoroughly happy married to two other people. He disagreed: "By any other arrangement," he said, "four people would have been unhappy instead of two."

"If you find so much that is unworthy of reverence in the United States then why do you live there," an interviewer asked **H. L. Mencken.**
His answer: "Why do men go to zoos?"

Walter Stone was one of the talented writers who created *The Jackie Gleason Show.* The pressure of working for Gleason led him to occasionally drink heavily. On one occasion he walked into a Les Vegas bar and asked for a double Scotch. "At eight in the morning?" asked the bartender incredulously.
"All right," said Stone. "Put a cornflake in it."

Olin Downes was a young music critic on *The Boston Post*, a paper with few pretensions. He submitted an article, in which he used the word "increment." His editor was outraged. How, the boss demanded, could Downes have used such foul language in a newspaper.
"You mean excrement," Downes explained.
"Increment, excrement, Downes. It's all shit to the readers of the *Boston Post.*"

William Randolph Hearst was very pleased with the work done by columnist **Arthur Brisbane.** In an effort to reward him, Hearst offered a six-month vacation, with all expenses paid. Brisbane said no. Hearst asked why.

"First of all, I'm afraid," said Brisbane, "that if I quit for six months the circulation of your newspapers may go down. And secondly, I'm afraid it may not."

Artist **James McNeill Whistler** was not always prompt in paying his bills. Once, while being visited by a gentleman to whom he owed money, he offered a glass of champagne.

"How," asked the creditor, "can you afford champagne, when you cannot even pay my bill?"

Said Whistler, "My dear man, let me assure you. I haven't paid for this, either."

When a fan exclaimed to Whistler that there were only two great painters in the world, "you and Velasquez," Whistler was contained in his modesty.

"Madam," he asked, "why drag in Valasquez?"

Picasso's famous painting *Guernica* is one of the most powerful expressions of destruction and man's inhumanity to man ever committed to canvas. Once, while Picasso was living in Paris during World War II, a Nazi officer visited his apartment and came across a photograph of the painting. "Did you do that?" he inquired.

"No," retorted the artist. "You did."

Eero Saarinen, the Finnish-American architect, spoke very slowly, which frustrated a television interviewer.

"Can't you speak a little more quickly?" he asked Saarinen.

"No sir. But I could say less."

"Is it hard to paint a picture?" a fan once asked **Salvador Dali.**

"No. It's either easy or impossible."

12

Ha Ha Ha

What gives us a taste for witty comebacks? Perhaps it's the kind of joke that **Henny Youngman** *specializes in, consisting of a setup and a topper.*

"Who was that lady I saw you with last night?" Youngman asks himself.

"That was no lady, that was my wife," he answers.

Few comedians besides Youngman even try to get laughs with many of these old chestnuts—though many of them still retain a certain charm. Then there was the one about the man who walked into a restaurant and . . .

Diner: "Do you serve wild rice here?"
Waiter: "No, we serve tame rice and mush it around till it gets mad."

Diner: "Do you serve crabs here?"
Waiter: "Certainly, but try to cheer up."

Diner: "Is there any soup on the menu?"
Waiter: "There was, but I wiped it off."

Diner: "What's this fly doing in my soup?"
Waiter: "I think it's the backstroke."

Diner: "Waiter, there's a fly in my soup."
Waiter: "That's all right mister, he won't drink much."

Diner: "Waiter, there's a fly in my soup."
Waiter: "Oh darn, I mixed up my orders again."

Diner: "Waiter, there's a fly in my soup."
Waiter: "Shhh! Not so loud. All the other customers will want one."

Diner: "Waiter, there's a fly in my soup."
Waiter: "What do you want for two dollars? An elephant?"

Diner: "Waiter, there's a fly in my soup."
Waiter: "If you wanted it with your dessert, you should have said so."

Jim: "How is your wife?"
Jeff: "Compared to who?"

The small-town prosecutor was hectoring the accused: "Listen, we have five witnesses who saw you steal that horse."

Replied the defendant: "Oh yeah? Well I have twenty witnesses who didn't see me take it."

"I can't bear a fool," the pompous lawyer told his client.

"Perhaps. But your mother could," responded the client.

The doctor said to his patient, "Listen, I know your heartbeat is a bit slow, but it doesn't worry me."

"Thanks," came the retort, "if your heartbeat was slow, it wouldn't worry me, either."

Joyce: "I got a necktie for my husband."
Belle: "Gee, I wish I could get such a good trade-in."

"Remember," explained the arresting officer, "whatever you say can and will be held against you."

"Cindy Crawford."

Mr. Burns: "Was that your wife who let me in?"

Mr. Fitz: "Would I hire a maid who looked like that?"

Man in dentist chair: "Yowch! You've just pulled the wrong tooth."

Dentist: "Relax. I'm coming to it."

A Floridian visiting California picked up a melon and asked, "Tell me, is this the largest apple you can grow in your state?"

Replied a native, "Oh, stop fingering that grape."

Train conductor: "Excuse me, mister, do you want to go to Bridgeport?"

Man on train: "No, I have to."

Professor: "A fool can ask more questions than a wise man can answer."

Student: "No wonder so many of us flunk your exams."

Young man: "The first time you contradict me, I'm going to kiss you."

Young lady: "No, you're not."

An executive from Steinway explained, "You know, more than five thousand elephants a year go to make our piano keys."

The visitor retorted, "It's remarkable what those beasts can be trained to do."

Beggar: "I haven't had anything to eat in two days."

Woman: "I wish I had your will power."

Political boss: "I'm out of politics for good."

Voter: "Whose?"

Mitch: "I wouldn't want to be a widow's second husband."

Mike: "I'd rather be her second husband than her first."

Philosopher: "You can catch more flies with honey than you can with vinegar."

Poet: "Yes, but what are you going to do with a bunch of flies?"

A lawyer who had emerged victorious in an "unwinnable case" called his client. "Justice has triumphed," he crowed.

His client responded, "Appeal the case at once."

13

Courtrooms, Labs,
and Battlefields

You don't tend to think of Perry Mason, Albert Einstein, or Alexander the Great as making witty repartee. But lawyers, scientists, and military figures have contributed some of the choicest bits of spontaneous commentary. Some of these offerings even include a bit of important life philosophy as when the **Duke of Wellington** *was asked by a young military man to share a piece of wisdom that would apply to his life in the armed forces.*

Explained the Duke, "Piss when you can."

Napoleon grew weary of complaints that one of his more unpopular commanders could attribute his successes to nothing more than luck.

"Then get me more lucky generals," retorted Napoleon.

Sick of hearing that Saddam Hussein was a brilliant tactician, Desert Storm General **H. Norman Schwarzkopf** argued, "As far as Saddam Hussein being a great military strategist, he is neither a strategist nor is he schooled in the operational art nor is he a tactician nor is he a general nor is he a soldier. Other than that, he's a great military man."

Thomas Edison much preferred laboring in his workshop to socializing. One time he was captured into attending a formal dinner. He finally made his way to the door and was desperate to escape, when the host attempted to snare him into a new conversation, "What are you working on now?" he asked.

"My exit," said Edison.

Niels Bohr was a Danish physicist who won the Nobel Prize in 1922 and later helped develop the atomic bomb for the United States. He had a horseshoe hanging on the wall of his home and a visitor was surprised: "Can it be that you of all people believe it will bring you luck?" he was asked.

"Of course not," said Bohr. "But I understand it brings you luck whether you believe in it or not."

J. B. Haldane was a brilliant British scientist. He was asked what inference could be drawn "about the nature of God from a study of His works?"

Haldane: "An inordinate fondness for beetles."

The great Supreme Court Justice **Benjamin Cardozo** began to feel ill during a boat outing. A colleague, noticing that the justice was turning green, asked him if he needed any help.

"Yes," said Cardozo. "Overrule the motion."

Robert Maynard Hutchins was dean of Yale Law School in the late 1920s. He was chatting with William Howard Taft, then chief justice of the Supreme Court. "I suppose you teach all your students that the judges are all fools," said Taft caustically.

"No, we let them find that out for themselves," replied Hutchins.

Adolphe A. Berle Jr. was assistant secretary of state under FDR and an influential adviser to the president. When still a student at Harvard Law School, Berle took Felix Frankfurter's famous course about public utilities. He completed the course successfully. So it was only natural for Frankfurter to be surprised when Berle began showing up in his classroom again, the following year.

"Weren't you in this class last year?" asked Frankfurter.

"Yes."

"Then why are you back?"

"I wanted to see if you had learned anything since last year," was the reply.

The Scopes trial, of course, centered around a schoolteacher who taught about evolution in his classroom. It pitted great orators Clarence Darrow and **William Jennings Bryan** against one another in a historic courtroom contest. Darrow repeatedly sought to punch holes in Bryan's fundamentalist belief that the Bible was the only source needed about the creation of the world. At one point, after establishing that God had created Adam and Eve and that Adam and Eve had brought forth Cain and Abel, Darrow asked, "Did you ever discover where Cain got his wife?"

"No sir," replied Bryan. "I leave the agnostics to hunt for her."

During the entire course of the so-called "Monkey Trial," Bryan repeatedly called **Clarence Darrow** an "agnostic," as though that were a crime.

Retorted Darrow, "I do not consider it an insult, but rather a compliment to be called an agnostic. I do not pretend to know, where many ignorant men are sure."

Supreme Court Justice **David H. Souter** was startled by a blistering dissenting opinion of fellow Justice Antonin Scalia.

"Justice Scalia's dissent is certainly the work of a gladiator," wrote Souter, "but he thrusts at lions of his own imagining."

14

Golden Nuggets from the Vast Wasteland

If only we could all be as witty as any six-year-old on a situation comedy. Life would be a regular laugh fest. Sadly, we don't have teams of highly paid writers helping us out. So many of us are left to vicariously enjoy the instantaneous wit that pours forth from the tube.

Lucy Ricardo was bragging about a homemade dress to her friend and confidante Ethel Mertz on the unforgettable *I Love Lucy*.

"I made it with my own hands," said Lucy.

"It looks like you made it with your own feet," commented Ethel.

Lucy hadn't told Ricky that she was pregnant—or expecting—as the early television censors forced them to express it. Ricky, meanwhile, was lecturing her, "You think you know how tough my job is, but believe me, if you traded places with me, you'd be surprised."

Lucy: "Believe me, if I traded places with you, you'd be surprised."

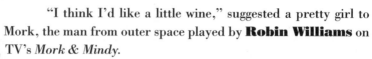

"I think I'd like a little wine," suggested a pretty girl to Mork, the man from outer space played by **Robin Williams** on TV's *Mork & Mindy*.

"All right, if you insist," replied the literal-minded Mork. "WAAAAAA."

George Burns to **Gracie Allen** on their television program: "Gracie, what do you think of television?"

Gracie: "I think it's wonderful. I hardly ever watch radio any more."

"Let's play horsey," offered father Danny Thomas on *Make Room for Daddy*.

"Okay," said his daughter Terry, a streetwise TV child, "Here's two dollars. Put it on Count Flash in the seventh."

Fred Sanford, played by the late Redd Foxx on television's *Sanford and Son*, was up in arms. "I still want to sow some wild oats!" he maintained.

"At your age," explained son Lamont, "you don't have no wild oats—you got shredded wheat!"

The television show *Roseanne* is a collection of verbal toppers held together by plot twists. When **Roseanne's** television daughter Becky complained, "Mom, you're neglecting me," Roseanne replied, "Don't take it personal. I'm neglecting your brother and sister, too."

On another occasion, a drunk in the Lobo Bar addressed Roseanne, who was working as a barmaid. "I could use another . . ." he began.

"What? Another liver?" she cut in.

Colonel Potter on the long-running comedy *M*A*S*H* asked a rhetorical question and received a less than rhetorical answer from Hawkeye as played by **Alan Alda.**

Potter: "By the way—what war is this?"

Hawkeye: "The latest war to end all wars."

Mary Richards, played by Mary Tyler Moore, was lecturing her good friend Rhoda about the importance of self-esteem. "I don't say that I am nothing," she explained.

"Sure," shot back Rhoda. "But you don't have to worry about someone beating you to it."

Felix Unger on the television version of *The Odd Couple* was describing his idea of the perfect date to his roommate Oscar: "I like my women quiet, ladylike, attractive, and refined."

Oscar: "What for?"

Leave It to Beaver's all-American Mom, June, was complaining to Ward, *Leave It to Beaver*'s incredibly wise Dad, about their son Wally's friends.

"You know," she said, "it's too bad we can't pick out a friend for Wally, some nice boy with all the right qualities who always behaves himself."

Said Ward, "The only trouble is, if we did find a boy like that, he probably wouldn't have anything to do with Wally."

Ralph and Alice, Ed and Trixie were always topping one another on the great TV sitcom *The Honeymooners*. Barely an episode went by when the unsuspecting Ralph, played by Jackie Gleason, wasn't one-upped by someone on the subject of his girth. A small sample:

> **Ralph** (bragging about a make-a-million idea): "This is probably the biggest thing I ever got into."
>
> **Alice:** "The biggest thing you ever got into was your pants."

Ralph: "I promise you this, Norton. I'm gonna learn. I'm gonna learn from here on in how to swallow my pride."

Norton: "That ought not to be too hard. You've learned how to swallow everything else."

Ralph: "Six hundred dollars is peanuts! What am I going to do with peanuts?"

Alice: "Eat them—like any other elephant."

Ralph: "If you see me coming down the street, get on the other side."

Norton: "When you come down the street, there ain't no other side."

Ralph: "You're the only man who turns my stomach upside down."

Norton: "There ain't a man in New York City that's strong enough to turn your stomach upside down."

Ralph: "You ain't talking me out of it, Alice. I'm going for that pot of gold."

Alice: "Just go for the gold—you've already got the pot."

Phil Silvers played Sergeant Bilko on the television comedy *The Phil Silvers Show*. When "the Sarge" was scheming, nobody else stood a chance. So when one private swore revenge, stating that "Bilko'll get his," the answer was obvious: "Oh. He's already got his. And he's got yours, too."

Miss Brooks, as played by the inimitable **Eve Arden,** lusted, for absolutely no good reason, after boring biology teacher Mr. Boynton. On one occasion they were arranging for a meal at Miss Brooks's house. "I'm not fussy," he told her. "I'll love whatever you put on my plate. I'll be there at seven."

"Fine," said Miss Brooks, eyes twinkling. "I'll be on your plate."

"What has she got that I haven't got?" asked Marion, the attractive female ghost on the TV situation situation comedy *Topper*.

The answer was simple to George, her phantom companion. "Visibility."

The Dick Van Dyke Show was jammed with verbal jousting. Whenever Richard Deacon, who played the basso profundo producer Mel Cooley, encountered **Morey Amsterdam,** who held the part of the joke-machine comedy writer Buddy Sorrell, sparks were sure to fly. Most often, Sorrell got the better of his boss. In fact, Mel had only one stock-in trade comeback for Buddy: "Yech!"

Mel: "Rob, I just left Alan's office."
Buddy: "I wish you just left this one."

Rob *(Dick Van Dyke)*: "Jim Darling . . . excuse me for staring at you. But I know I know you."
Mel: "Well, of course you do. He's one of our nation's most dynamic businessmen."
Buddy: "Thataboy, Mel. Keep a civil tongue on his boot."

Mel: (accepting an invitation to a party): "What time would you like me to be there, Rob?"
Buddy: "How about just as we're leaving."

Rob: "Hold it a minute, you guys. All Mel said is there's a change in the show. Maybe the change will make you happy."
Buddy: "The only change that would make me happy would be the firing of all hairless producers that look like potbellied penguins."

Rob: "Would you save the insults, please?"
Buddy: "What for? Mel's here now."

Rob: "What's the big problem?"
Mel: "It's about the guest spot. We just lost Sophia Loren."
Buddy: "How could anybody lose Sophia Loren?"

15

Hollywood Zingers

Scarlett O'Hara is once again hysterical, nearly sobbing, pleading with an unmoved **Rhett Butler** *as the background music swells, "Rhett, Rhett! Rhett, if you go where shall I go? What shall I do?"*

But Butler's love for the selfish O'Hara is gone—just like the Old South. "Frankly my dear," he intones. "I don't give a damn."

It doesn't get much better than that. But it often gets pretty darn good, when Hollywood turns its deft hand toward the lyrical retort.

FROM *ADAM'S RIB* (1949):

Amanda Bonner *(Katharine Hepburn):* "So, what I said was true; there's no difference between the sexes. Men. Women. The same."

Adam Bonner *(Spencer Tracy):* "They are, huh?"

Amanda: "Well, maybe there is a difference, but it's a little difference."

Adam: [Laughs] "Well, you know as the French say . . ."

Amanda: "What do they say?"

Adam: "Vive la difference."

Amanda: "Which means?

Adam: "Which means: Hurray for that little difference."

FROM *AN AMERICAN IN PARIS* (1951):

Gene Kelly plays Jerry Mulligan, a young American painting student in France. In this scene he discusses the attire of Milo Roberts, played by Nina Foch.

> **Jerry Mulligan:** "That's . . . uh . . . quite a dress you almost have on."
> **Milo Roberts:** "Thanks!"
> **Mulligan:** "What holds it up?"
> **Roberts:** "Modesty."

FROM *CAPTAINS COURAGEOUS* (1937):

The gentle fisherman Manuel, played by Spencer Tracy, is talking to his young friend Harvey, portrayed by Freddie Bartholomew.

> **Harvey:** "You think they really fish in heaven?"
> **Manuel:** "Why sure, they fish in heaven. What else they do? The apostles, they all fishermen, ain't they?"

FROM *A DAY AT THE RACES* (1937):

> **Flor** *(Esther Muer):* "Hold me closer, closer, closer."
> **Hugo Z. Hackenbush** *(Groucho Marx):* "If I hold you any closer, I'll be in back of you."

FROM *A NIGHT AT THE OPERA* (1935):

Otis B. Driftwood *(Groucho Marx):* "It's all right, tha-that's in every contract. Tha-that's what they call a sanity clause."

Fiorello *(Chico Marx):* [Laughs] "You can't fool me, there ain't no sanity clause!"

FROM *DINNER AT EIGHT* (1933):

Kitty Packard, played by the glamorous Jean Harlow, is a character who never has trouble attracting men—even at a distance.

Kitty Packard: "I was reading a book the other day."

Carlotta Vance *(Marie Dressler):* "Reading a book?"

Kitty: "Yes, it's all about civilization or something. A nutty kind of a book. Do you know that the guy said that machinery is going to take the place of every profession?"

Carlotta: "Oh, my dear. That's something you need never worry about."

FROM *KING KONG* (1933):

Police Captain *(George MacQuarrie):* "Well, Denham, the airplanes got him!"

Carl Denham *(Robert Armstrong):* "Oh no. It wasn't the airplanes. It was beauty killed the beast."

FROM *LOVE AT FIRST BITE* (1979):

Renfield *(Arte Johnson):* "But master, you're Dracula, son of Drakul. You've been the reigning Prince of Darkness for over seven hundred glorious years."

Dracula *(George Hamilton):* "Seven hundred lonely years, Renfield."

Renfield: "Lonely, master? Lonely? But I thought you were happy living—I mean dying—I mean existing—all those years. I . . . I thought you were having fun."

Dracula: "Fun? How would you like to go around dressed like a headwaiter for the last seven hundred years?"

FROM *THE NIGHT OF THE IGUANA* (1964):

Hannah Jelkes *(Deborah Kerr):* "There are worse things than chastity, Mr. Shannon."

T. Lawrence Shannon *(Richard Burton):* "Yes—lunacy and death."

FROM *SOME LIKE IT HOT* (1959):

Jerry/Daphne *(Jack Lemmon):* "Well, ya don't understand, Osgood."

Osgood E. Fielding III *(Joe E. Brown):* "Yeah?"

Jerry/Daphne: "I'm a man."

Osgood: "Well, nobody's perfect!"

FROM *THE SUNSHINE BOYS* (1975):

Willy Clark *(Walter Matthau):* "Ahh, you're a funny man, Al—a pain in the ass, but a funny man."

Al Lewis *(George Burns):* "Y'know what your trouble was, Willy. You always took the jokes too seriously. They were just jokes. We did comedy on the stage for forty-three years and I don't think you enjoyed it once."

Clark: "If I was there to enjoy it, I would buy a ticket."

FROM *THE THIN MAN* (1934):

Detective Nick Charles *(William Powell)* talks over his eventful day with his wife Nora, played by Myrna Loy.

Nick Charles: "Oh, I'm a hero. I was shot twice in the *Tribune.*"

Nora Charles: "I read where you were shot five times in the tabloids."

Nick: "It's not true . . . he didn't come anywhere near my tabloids."

FROM *THE LION KING* (1994):
Simba: "Hey, Uncle Scar, when I'm king what'll that make you?"
Scar: "A monkey's uncle!"

16

Leaders, Thinkers, Politicians, and a Few Scoundrels

Ask a friend if he can come up with a great example of a verbal comeback—any example—from all of history. Bet you a nickel, this is the one you'll hear:

Dan Quayle compared himself to John Kennedy in the vice presidential debates of 1988. Retorted his opponent **Lloyd Bentsen:** "Senator, I served with Jack Kennedy. I knew Jack Kennedy. Jack Kennedy was a friend of mine. Senator, you're no Jack Kennedy."

Though, this particular topper has found its way into the public's consciousness like none other, there are dozens of instances in which famous leaders, philosophers, and the like have fired off mighty retorts. Even members of the royal family have done so from time to time. Hardly a man or woman has ever lived who bested Winston Churchill on the verbal battlefield.

When political satirist **Mark Russell** heard Bentsen's crack about Dan Quayle being no John Kennedy, he had an addendum, "Hell, he's no Caroline Kennedy."

Toward the end of his life, **Winston Churchill** visited the House of Commons. A buzz throughout the room accompanied his presence, taking away from attention to the debate at hand. "They say he's potty," murmured one member of Parliament.

"They say he can't hear either," murmured back Churchill.

George Bernard Shaw telegrammed Winston Churchill just prior to the opening of *Major Barbara:* "Have reserved two tickets for first night. Come and bring a friend if you have one."

Churchill wired back, "Impossible to come to first night. Will come to second night, if you have one."

When a critic complained that Churchill had ended a sentence with a preposition, the prime minister replied, "This is the sort of English up with which I will not put."

A rather rude American woman practically assaulted Winston Churchill at a reception, demanding to know, "What are you going to do about those wretched Indians?"

Said Churchill: "To which Indians do you refer? Do you refer to the second greatest nation on earth, which under benign and munificent

British rule has multiplied and prospered accordingly? Or to the unfortunate North American Indians, which under your present administration are almost extinct?"

"Are you trying to set me on fire?" Russian leader **Nikita Khrushchev** asked John Kennedy, when an errant match fell behind his chair.

"Of course not."

"Ah," bellowed the Soviet leader. "A capitalist, not an incendiary."

Khrushchev was delivering a speech before a large audience, in which he denounced the flaws of the Stalin regime.

From the audience came the voice of a heckler. "You were one of Stalin's colleagues! Why didn't you stop him?"

Khrushchev paused and stared into the audience. "Who said that?" he bellowed angrily.

Silence reigned, as no one answered.

"Now," said Khrushchev in a firm, quiet voice, "you know why."

President Kennedy was praising **Arthur Goldberg,** then secretary of labor, for effectively halting a looming labor strike.

Goldberg didn't feel that he deserved the praise. Said he, "The trick is to be there when it's settled."

Golda Meir, prime minister of Israel, wanted nothing more than peace with the Arabs. But she insisted that she could never achieve that goal without meeting her enemies face to face across the bargaining table. A journalist challenged her: "Even divorces are arranged without personal confrontation," he said.

"I'm not interested in a divorce," she replied. "I'm interested in a marriage."

Congressmen were livid over the fact that the CIA had placed mines in Nicaraguan harbors. They raked **Tony Motley,** Assistant Secretary of State for Inter-American Affairs, over the coals for the action.

"This is terrible," one legislator said. "We're involved in illegal, covert actions, and we're killing sailors from other countries."

"Just a minute," Motley shot back. "Let me put this thing in context. Fewer people were killed by these mines than died in Chappaquiddick."

Senator Ted Kennedy is a passionate supporter of the rights of foreigners with AIDS to come to live in the United States. He made a speech to that effect, and senatorial adversary **Jesse Helms** shot back, "Let me adjust my hearing aid. It could not accommodate the decibels of the senator from Massachusetts. I can't match him in decibels or Jezebels, or anything else, apparently."

Connecticut governor **Lowell P. Weicker** had a rather public feud with millionaire Donald J. Trump in late 1993. Trump had made some comments about Native Americans who owned casinos, and the governor accused the rich man of bigotry.

Things heated up from there, with Trump announcing that Weicker was "a dirtbag . . . a fat slob who couldn't get elected dog catcher in Connecticut."

Weicker retorted, "I can lose weight a lot faster than a bigot can lose bigotry!"

Joe DioGuardi was the first practicing CPA ever elected to Congress, in 1984. He had run promising to use his number skills to ferret out budgetary gimmicks in the government. But his first meeting with Republican party leaders was a bit disillusioning. "Joe," said one, "you're in Washington now, and it's time you put away your green eyeshades."

"With all due respect, sir," the new congressman replied, "I'm not going to trade in my green eyeshades for your blinders."

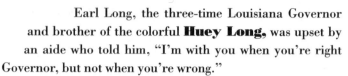

Earl Long, the three-time Louisiana Governor and brother of the colorful **Huey Long,** was upset by an aide who told him, "I'm with you when you're right Governor, but not when you're wrong."

Retorted Long: "You stupid son of a bitch, I don't need you when I'm right."

After Exxon's *Valdez* fouled many miles of Alaskan coastline with an enormous oil spill, critics wanted to blame someone, but had difficulty deciding who—Exxon or the ship's captain, a man who admitted to having problems with alcohol.

A defender of the oil firms took up the defense in the Alaska legislature. "Twenty-five years ago," he said, "Alaska suffered an act of God—the Good Friday earthquake. We didn't waste time seeking to punish the cause of that disaster."

"As far as I know," retorted Alaska State Senate President **Tim Kelly,** "God wasn't drunk when the earthquake hit."

Ann Richards was Texas state treasurer before she was governor of the Lone Star State. On one occasion, she was consulted about the religious object on the grounds of the capitol building.

"What do you think about the crèche—does it have to go?"

Richards's reply: "Oh, I hate to see them take that crèche out of the capitol. It could be the only chance we'll ever have to get three wise men in that building."

Austrian statesman **Prince Metternich** was known as the ultimate diplomat. His actions were always based on careful thought and analysis of their consequences. Once, an aide entered a meeting to breathlessly announce, "The Russian ambassador has just dropped dead."

Metternich thought aloud, "I wonder what his motivation could have been."

No love has been lost between Senator Jesse Helms and Senator **Carol Moseley-Braun.** When they met in the senate elevator, Helms looked at his companion, Orrin Hatch, and said, "I'm going to make her cry. I'm going to sing 'Dixie' until she cries."

Moseley-Braun looked directly at Helms and shot back, "Senator Helms, your singing would make me cry if you sang 'Rock of Ages.'"

"Would **Mr. Yeltsin** like to see some pigs?" an American host asked the Russian leader.

"I'd prefer to see some Americans," Yeltsin answered. "But pigs will do."

Dr. **Benjamin Baker Moeur** was governor of Arizona in the early 1930s. He was fond of praising his wife by telling her, "Honey, you're getting better looking all the time."

"Thanks," she once answered. "I wish I could say the same for you."

"You could, if you were as good a liar as I am."

The 1948 presidential election was very close. In fact, when the candidates went to bed, it appeared that Thomas E. Dewey had vanquished his rival Harry Truman. As they prepared for bed, Dewey asked his wife, "How will it be to sleep with the President of the United States?"

"A high honor, and quite frankly, darling, I'm looking forward to it."

By the next morning, the news was out, and Mrs. Dewey looked her husband in the eye and asked, "Tell me Tom, am I going to Washington or is Harry coming here?"

Lord John Russell, the British statesman, was asked what he thought would be the proper punishment for a bigamist. "Two mothers-in-law," was his answer.

Samuel May was a well-known abolitionist of the pre–Civil War era. He encountered **Susan B. Anthony,** the early feminist. "You have no business to be discussing marriage," he told her. "You are not married."

Countered Anthony, "You, Mr. May, are not a slave. Suppose you quit lecturing on slavery."

Moshe Dayan, the Israeli foreign minister and minister of defense, was known worldwide for his eye patch. When he was pulled over by a military policeman for speeding, Dayan responded, "I have only one eye. What do you want me to watch—the speedometer or the road?"

Will Rogers Jr. was a CBS television announcer. He was interviewing **Adlai Stevenson,** but got a little bollixed up when he ended the interview by saying, "Thank you very much Governor Harriman."

Stevenson didn't let the faux pas pass. "Goodbye, Dave Garroway," he said, using the name of the *Today Show* host.

Daniel O'Connell, an Irish Roman Catholic leader in the British House of Commons, viciously attacked Prime Minister **Benjamin Disraeli** one day, going so far as to assault Disraeli for his Jewish heritage.

Disraeli responded, "Yes, I am a Jew, and when the ancestors of the right honorable gentleman were brutal savages in an unknown island, mine were priests in the temple of Solomon."

French novelist and dramatist **Jean Giraudoux** served as French minister of information in the years before World War I. One of the primary difficulties the nations faced at the time was rising unemployment.

"If things go on this way another year, we'll all be begging," claimed one of the nation's leaders.

"From whom?" inquired Giraudoux.

In early 1995 a great brouhaha broke out when House Majority leader Dick Armey was alleged to have called gay Democratic Representative **Barney Frank** "Barney Fag." Armey later claimed it was only an innocent slip of the tongue.

"I rule out that it was an innocent mispronunciation," replied Frank. "I turned to my own expert, my mother, who reports that in fifty-nine years of marriage no one ever introduced her as Elsie Fag."

"Who will come after you?" British leader **Margaret Thatcher** was asked.

"After me," she said, "there's me!"

"The Lord is out walking in the park," explained Lord Beaverbrook's valet.

"On the waters, I suppose," suggested **Randolph Churchill,** Winston's son.

"I never give way to scoundrels," stated John Randolph as he walked toward his longtime political enemy, **Henry Clay.**

Clay stood aside. "I always do," he said.

Warren Robinson Austin was the U.S. delegate to the United Nations in the years following World War II. Once he was asked whether he found the endless speechifying at the U.N. boring.

"Yes I do," said Austin. "But it is better for aged diplomats to be bored than for young men to die."

In the middle years of the eighteenth century, the citizens of Pennsylvania were threatened by the French. **Benjamin Franklin** set about encouraging the Pennsylvanians to support their new militia. One well-off man was hesitant. "Frankly," he asked, "why should I help to save Quakers who won't fight to defend themselves?"

Said Franklin, "You're like the sailor who won't caulk the leaky ship because it would save the rats."

Benjamin Franklin was having a pleasant evening at a tavern in Philadelphia, discussing the Declaration of Independence. A young man who had been drinking too much advanced on Franklin's table angrily. "Them words don't mean nothing at all," he shouted. "Where's all the happiness that document says it guarantees us?"

Franklin: "My friend, the declaration only guarantees the American people the right to pursue happiness. You have to catch it yourself!"

When a journalist suggested that the Princesses would soon leave England, in the wake of the World War II bombing of Buckingham Palace, **Elizabeth** (then the king's consort, now the Queen Mother) was firm: "The children will not leave unless I do. I shall not leave unless their father does, and the King will not leave the country in any circumstances whatever."

Princess Anne ran into a gentleman at an equestrian event in England. "Has anyone ever told you that you look like Princess Anne?" he said, not recognizing her.

"I think I'm a bit better looking than she is," the Princess responded.

Queen Victoria was only twenty-one when she gave birth to her first child. As the baby was born, the queen's physician proudly exclaimed, "Oh Madam, it is a princess."

The queen was quick in her response: "Never mind," said she, "the next will be a prince." (It was.)

Sigmund Freud was unfazed by the criticisms of contemporaries. A colleague, Sandor Firenczi, came to him one day, upset by the fact that so many so-called experts were trying to punch holes into Freud's theories. "Don't worry so much, Sandor," said Freud. "Surely our opponents deride our theories by day. But they dream according to them at night."

Polly Adler ran a famous New York house of ill repute for many years. Once, when briefly incarcerated, she was asked to comment on life in jail. "I don't mind the work," she said, "but the hours aren't good."

When asked why he robbed banks, **Willie Sutton** had the logical answer: "Because that's where the money is."

Alexander the Great conquered most of the known world in his lifetime. Yet the philosopher **Diogenes the Cynic** was not overly impressed. Alexander visited the philosopher and asked if there were anything the old man wanted of him.

"Yes," Diogenes replied, "Get out from between me and the sun."

"What is the best kind of death?" asked a friend of **Julius Caesar.**

"A sudden one," said Caesar, who certainly got his wish.

Acknowledgments

The search for comebacks is endless; there's always the feeling that the next book, newspaper, or magazine will be a treasure trove. Here are some of the outstanding sources, which were of invaluable help in assembling this collection:

The Little Brown Book of Anecdotes, edited by Clifton Fadiman, Little, Brown and Company, 1985; *The Oxford Book of Literary Anecdotes,* edited by James Sutherland, Touchstone, 1975; *Dictionary of Quotations,* Bergan Evans, Avenel, 1978; *Quotable Business,* Louis E. Boone, Random House, 1992; *The Great TV Sit-Com Book,* Rick Mitz, Richard Marek Publishers, 1980; *Quotable Sex,* Carole McKenzie, St. Martin's Press, 1992; *The Vicious Circle,* Margaret Case Harriman, Rinehart & Co., Inc., 1951; *Barbed Wires,* edited by Joyce Denebrink, Simon & Schuster, 1965; *The Wit and Wisdom of Abraham Lincoln,* edited by Alex Ayres, Meridian, 1992; *The American Annual,* Grolier Incorporated, 1989; *Shake Well Before Using,* Bennett Cerf, Simon & Schuster, 1948; *Good for a Laugh,* Bennett Cerf, Hanover House, 1952; *The Uncommon Wisdom of Jacqueline Kennedy Onassis,* edited by Bill Adler, Citadel Press, 1994; *From the Movies,* Richard Griffith and Arthur Mayer, Simon & Schuster, 1957; *Dorothy Parker: What Fresh Hell Is This,* Marion Meade, Villard Books, 1988; *Wit's End: Days and Nights of the Algonquin Round Table,* James R. Gaines, Harcourt Brace Jovanovich, 1977; *The Time of Laugher,* Corey Ford, Little, Brown, 1967; *George S. Kaufman, an Intimate Portrait,* Howard Teichman, Atheneum, 1972; *10,000 Jokes, Toasts and Stories,* edited by Lewis and Faye Copeland,

Garden City Books, 1939; *How Did They Die?* Norman and Betty Donaldson, Green-wich House, 1980; *Go East Young Man: The Autobiography of William O. Douglas,* Random House, 1974; *Just Tell Me When to Cry,* Richard Fleischer, Carroll & Graf, 1993; *A Very Human President,* Jack Valenti, Norton, 1975; *A Thousand Days,* Arthur M. Schlesinger, Jr., Houghton Mifflin, 1965; *Familiar Quotations,* John Bartlett, Fourteenth Edition, Little Brown; *The Wit and Wisdom of Mark Twain,* edited by Alex Ayres, Meridian, 1989; *Will the Gentleman Yield?* Bill Hogan and Mike Hill, Ten Speed Press, 1987; *The 776 Nastiest Things Ever Said,* Ross and Kathryn Petras, Harper Perennial, 1995; *The Wit & Wisdom of Benjamin Franklin,* James C. Humes, HarperCollins, 1995; *Citizen Hearst,* W. A. Swanberg, Charles Scribner's Sons, 1961; *As FDR Said,* Frank Kingdon, Duell, Sloan and Pearce, 1950; *In All His Glory,* Sally Bedell Smith, Simon & Schuster, 1990; *Growing Up with Chico,* Maxine Marx, Prentice Hall, 1980; *The Movies,* Richard Griffith and Arthur Mayer, Simon & Schuster, 1957; *Here's to the Friars,* Joey Adams, Crown, 1976; *Madame Sarah,* Cornelia Otis Skinner, Dell Publishing Company, 1966; *The Fabulous Showman: the Life and Times of P.T. Barnum,* Irving Wallace, Alfred A. Knopf, 1959; *Funny People,* Steve Allen, Stein and Day, 1981; *Tracy and Hepburn,* Garson Kanin, Viking, 1971; *The World According to Beaver,* Irwyn Applebaum, MCA Publishing, 1984; *The People's Almanac #2,* David Wallechinsky and Irving Wallace, William Morrow and Co., 1978; *The Wit and Wisdom of Winston Churchill,* James C. Humes, HarperCollins, 1994; *Baseball's Greatest Quotations,* Paul Dickson, HarperPerennial, 1991; *The Pleasure of Their Company,* Howard Taubman, Amadeus Press, 1994.

Back issues of the following newspapers and magazines were also invaluable in tracking down comebacks through the years: *Time, Newsweek, The New York Times, New York Newsday, Esquire, The Economist, Playboy, Reader's Digest, Forbes, Atlantic Monthly.*

With a bow toward the arrival of modern media, various CD-ROMs were also quite helpful, including Microsoft's *Cinemania,* Microsoft's *Encarta,* CNN *Newsroom Global View,* and *Time Almanac 1993.*

Thanks are in order, too, for the many men, women and children whom we enlisted (whether they knew it or not) in our hunt for blindingly witty repartee. A handful stand out. With apologies to those we may have missed, they include: Herbert Barrett, Helen Thurber, Bernardette Haken, Steven Fink, Kim Fader, and most especially Anne Mintz for giving us access to the electronic wonderland she oversees.

Finally, we'd like to reflect our appreciation to two other people: our editor Becky Cabaza, who was kind to us throughout the process and seemed to share our sometimes unusual sense of humor, and our agent, Stuart Krichevsky, who stands ever ready to protect us from people who are making us crazy.

To the Readers

Any readers who come across items that seem appropriate for future sequels to *"Frankly, My Dear..."* are invited to send them in. Like people everywhere who want something for nothing, the authors cannot guarantee credit—or even that there will be a sequel. However, clever readers with true generosity of spirit should feel free to send their contributions to "Frankly, My Dear...," 175 Fifth Avenue, Suite 2390, New York, New York 10010. The authors will guarantee a lovely thank you note, of the kind that would make their mothers proud, for any contributions that are actually used.